THE UNITED NATIONS
at 70

Restoration and Renewal

The Seventieth Anniversary of the United Nations
and the Restoration of the New York Headquarters

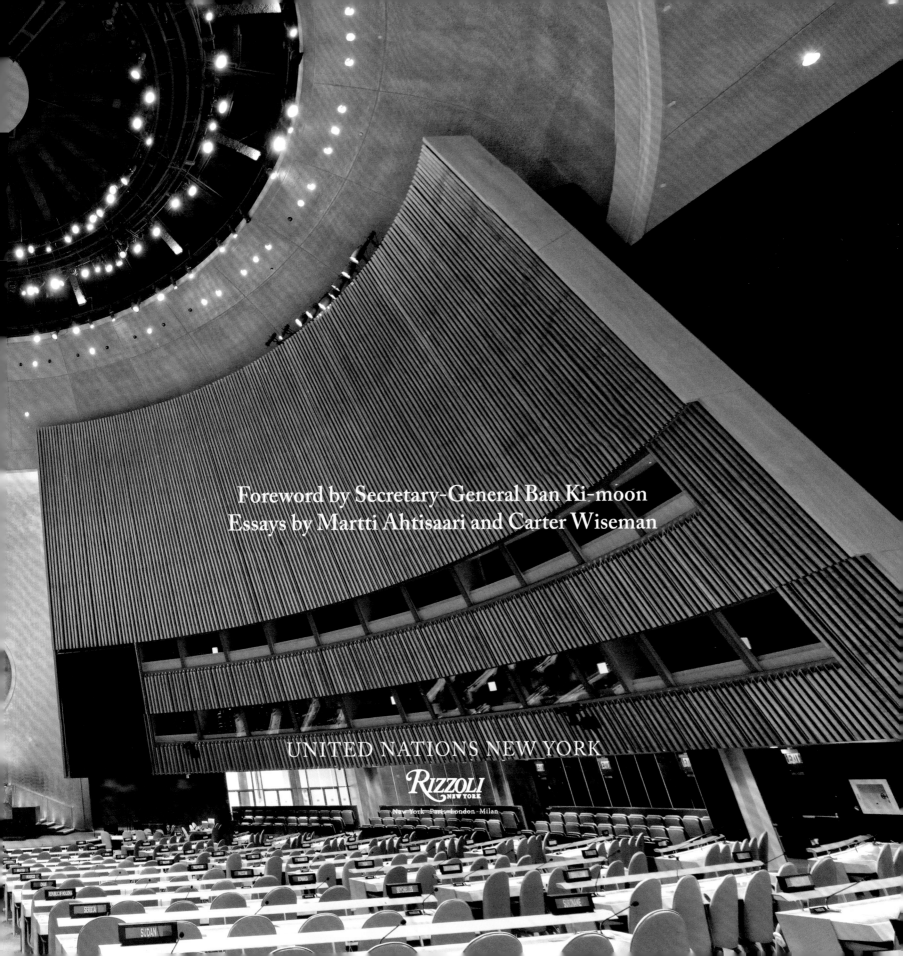

Foreword by Secretary-General Ban Ki-moon
Essays by Martti Ahtisaari and Carter Wiseman

UNITED NATIONS NEW YORK

RIZZOLI
NEW YORK

New York · Paris · London · Milan

First published in the United States of America in 2015 by
RIZZOLI INTERNATIONAL PUBLICATIONS, INC.
300 Park Avenue South, New York, NY 10010
www.rizzoliusa.com

ISBN-13: 978-0-8478-4615-3
Library of Congress Control Number: 2015935595

Distributed to the U.S. Trade by Random House,
New York

Edited by Andrea Monfried
Designed by Abigail Sturges Graphic Design

Printed and bound in China
2015 2016 2017 2018 2019 / 10 9 8 7 6 5 4 3 2 1

Contents

Foreword

SECRETARY-GENERAL BAN KI-MOON

The seventieth anniversary of the United Nations finds an organization with major achievements to its credit, daunting challenges ahead, and a dedicated staff striving to bring the ideals and objectives of the United Nations Charter to life. For seven decades, the United Nations has worked around the world and around the clock to confront the emergencies of the day while building the foundations for a better tomorrow. Peace, development, and human rights are the interrelated and mutually reinforcing pillars of our efforts.

We can look back on a proud record of working with many partners to dismantle colonialism, defeat smallpox, triumph over apartheid, advance international law, keep the peace in troubled areas, and articulate a body of treaties to safeguard every person's birthright to freedom, equality, and dignity. The United Nations is the world's first responder in times of disaster, its leading forum for the peaceful resolution of disputes, and its universal arena for global problem-solving and multilateral action for the common good.

From this vantage point of grave responsibility, we are keenly aware that conditions in today's world remain a far cry from the vision enshrined in the Charter. Armed conflict, displacement, and persecution are daily realities for millions. Hunger and exploitation afflict billions. Violence against women blights all societies. Huge amounts of money continue to be squandered on nuclear weapons and other destabilizing military arsenals. The consequences of climate change are ever more apparent—and have only just begun. And though the world said "never again" after the Holocaust, and once more after genocides in Cambodia, Rwanda, and Srebrenica, atrocious crimes have continued.

The seventieth anniversary of the United Nations comes at a time of great transition for the human family—one that offers a momentous opportunity to address these threats by mobilizing global action to secure our shared future. Urbanization and migration are on the rise. New economic powers are emerging. An organization founded with 51 Member States has nearly quadrupled in size and is now home to 193. A global population of an estimated 2.3 billion in 1945 has grown to more than 7 billion. Most of all, the distinctions between the national and the international are disappearing. In such an irreversibly interconnected world, challenges faced by one become challenges faced by all—sometimes gradually but often suddenly. That is the global logic of our times. With our

Secretary-General Ban Ki-moon visiting the construction site during the renovation of the United Nations Headquarters.

Ribbon-cutting ceremony marking the completed renovation of the Secretariat Building, 21 December 2012: Yukio Takasu, Under-Secretary-General for Management; Vuk Jeremić, President of the sixty-seventh session of the United Nations General Assembly; Ban Soon-taek; Secretary-General Ban Ki-moon; Ambassador Patrick Kennedy, United States Under-Secretary of State for Management; the Honorable Marjorie B. Tiven, Commissioner of the New York City Mayor's Office for International Affairs; Michael Adlerstein, Assistant Secretary-General and Executive Director of the Capital Master Plan (left to right).

fates ever more entwined, our future must be one of shared prosperity and ever deeper cooperation. A more connected world demands that nations become more united—and with a spirit of global citizenship that lives up to the promise of the organization's very name.

I am confident this is possible. I have seen it in my own life. My connection with the United Nations dates back to my boyhood in war-torn Korea. I was able to eat thanks to grain from UNICEF, learn thanks to textbooks from UNESCO, and feel safe thanks to the presence of soldiers from many nations operating under the blue United Nations flag. The United Nations was a symbol of international concern for our plight; we found great strength in knowing we were not alone. I want to bring that same sense of hope and solidarity to people in need today and to ensure that the United Nations is an effective instrument of progress and dignity for all. That is my seventieth-anniversary commitment to the world's people.

This volume depicts the renovation of the United Nations Headquarters complex in New York—the Capital Master Plan. With generous support from our Member States, offices, meeting rooms, and other facilities have been restored, renewed, and reinvented for the twenty-first century, while the rich heritage of architecture and design has been preserved. The United Nations is now a state-of-the-art institution where all partners can come together to improve the state of the world.

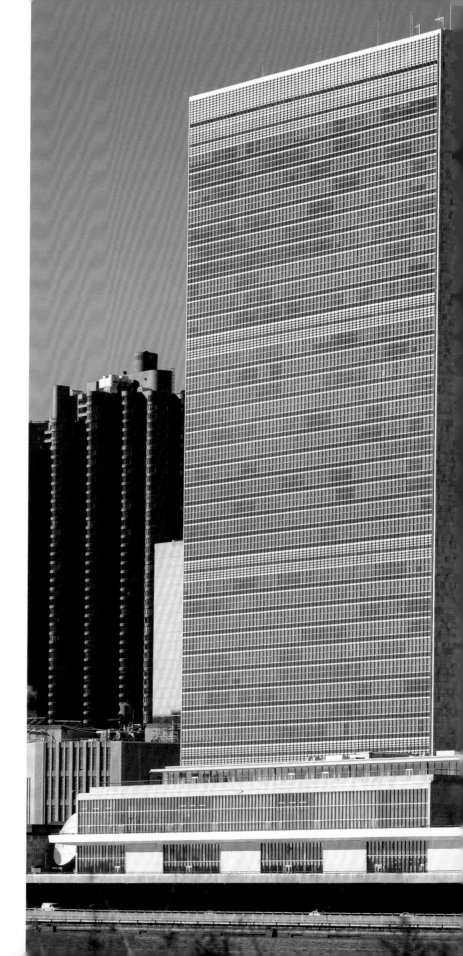

View of the United Nations Headquarters from the east, 2015. The Secretariat Building (left) stands above the low-rise Conference Building; the General Assembly Building (centre) and the temporary North Lawn Building (right) complete the panorama.

Personal Reflections
on the United Nations at Seventy

MARTTI AHTISAARI

Sometimes it is useful to ponder which of the many decisions concerning one's professional life has been the most significant. Which is the choice that has given direction to a career as a public actor? In my case, perhaps it was the decision to accept a junior appointment in the small and still nascent Bureau of Technical Assistance to Developing Countries in the Finnish Ministry for Foreign Affairs. That opened the path to a wider world and brought me into contact with the United Nations and the continent of Africa, where I have spent a fair part of my professional years. That choice was made in 1965.

In the years that followed, Denmark, Norway, Sweden, and Finland had plenty of cooperation in most fields of public life. Development cooperation was a new area for us: we had no colonial history to speak of. It would prove to be a most dynamic and creative field of work.

In 1973, I was appointed Ambassador to Tanzania, a country I had come to know during my years with the Finnish Foreign Ministry. I was also accredited to Zambia, Somalia, and later, to Mozambique. In those days, Tanzania was particularly interesting. First, the country was an arena for new social experiments. In addition, the African liberation movements, including the South West Africa People's Organization

(SWAPO), were hosted by the Government of Tanzania. It was my mission to be in close touch with those delegations, which in turn led to my being drafted to serve as United Nations Commissioner for Namibia, then a new candidate for United Nations membership. My assignment started in 1977. I had been a member of the senate of the United Nations Institute for Namibia—in Lusaka, Zambia—so I was no stranger to the new mission. Secretary-General Kurt Waldheim then appointed me as his Special Representative to Namibia.

The United Nations and Namibia's Road to Independence

It was impossible to foresee the dramatic developments looming on the horizon. My work was facilitated by the fact that I had met and come to know several of the key personalities of SWAPO who were also operating from the Frontline States (Angola, Botswana, Mozambique, Tanzania, Zambia, and Zimbabwe). The United Nations had adopted a nation-building programme for Namibia, and my efforts involved helping to facilitate its implementation. What the country needed most, in order to be well administered once the day of

Young girl carrying a pine seedling, Haiti, 2011. Haitian students commemorated World Environment Day 2011 by planting trees in a depleted forest near Port-au-Prince. Observed annually on 5 June, World Environment Day was established by the General Assembly in 1972 to raise worldwide awareness of environmental issues and to encourage political action.

RIGHT
Children in a Windhoek township, Namibia, 1989. The boys and girls are holding United Nations Transition Assistance Group bumper stickers that read, in Afrikaans, "Free and Fair Elections" during Namibia's transition to independence.

independence arrived, was a well-educated work force to lead the government. I am a strong believer in the power of education, and so the task was a particularly dear one for me.

The road to Namibian independence went through the United Nations Security Council, which adopted Resolution 435 in 1978. The resolution provided the framework for the Namibian independence process, but only as a matter of general principle. It was obvious that South Africa was not at all ready to give up its hold on Namibia. This situation led to a continuation of the armed struggle with SWAPO. The entire issue of an independent Namibia became a victim of the Cold War, with the pros and cons of independence interpreted through that particular prism. Years passed; the war continued.

December 1988 was a decisive moment in the progress towards Namibian independence. The United States mediation team, headed by Assistant Secretary of State for African Affairs Chester A. Crocker, brought negotiators from Angola, Cuba, and South Africa together, alongside observers from the Soviet Union, to facilitate the implementation of Resolution 435. For South Africa to accept the start of a United Nations monitoring mission in Namibia, we had to get an agreement with Angola and Cuba for the Cuban forces to withdraw from Angola. On 13 December, Cuba, South Africa, and Angola agreed to a total Cuban troop withdrawal from Angola. The Soviet Union and the Frontline States played a crucial role in this process.

Implementation of Resolution 435 officially began on 1 April 1989, when I arrived in Windhoek, Namibia, as head of the United Nations Transition Assistance Group. Hopes were high. Peace had prevailed, and it seemed as though the march towards independence would progress without serious incident. Therefore, the

news that large numbers of SWAPO fighters had crossed into Namibia from Angola was a shock to the international community. Conflict with South African forces meant that the agreed armistice was broken.

For the United Nations, the highest priority was to restore peace. The alternative was prolonged strife, perhaps even war, which would ruin all hopes for an early Namibian independence. South Africa was the only player present with forces adequate to stop SWAPO fighters. The United Nations presence was by far too small, and too poorly equipped, to be of use at that moment. Inviting South African forces to restore order was a highly controversial and risky decision, but that was simply what I had to do. Fully aware that I would expose myself to strong criticism, I realized that it was the only way to solve the problem.

The governments concerned understood that I had taken the decision in an emergency and without any real alternatives. It did not take long before the situation calmed down. However, international criticism of my actions continued. I never lost sight of the fact that the most important thing was to ensure that the continuation of sufficient conditions for the Namibian independence process could be secured.

As could be expected in such historic circumstances, the United Nations operation was massive: some 4,600 peacekeepers, 1,500 police officers, and 1,800 election observers from more than a hundred countries arrived for the national election held in November 1989. The administrative task was overwhelming. SWAPO won a landslide victory in the new parliament. The elections had been free and fair and constituted one of the United Nations' biggest achievements since its creation in 1945.

In retrospect, when I think about Namibia and the role of the United Nations, I realize that the experience was pivotal in reaching an

RIGHT
Girls in Darfur, Sudan, welcoming the arrival of a delegation from the African Union–United Nations Hybrid Operation in Darfur, 2012. The delegation celebrated the inauguration of projects focussing on education, sanitation, health, community development, and the empowerment of women.

LEFT
Villagers welcoming Secretary-General Ban Ki-moon to Kyauk Ka Char, Myanmar, 2012. Secretary-General Ban visited a drug alternative development project co-sponsored by Myanmar's government and the United Nations Office on Drugs and Crime. The scheme aims at providing farmers with an alternative to growing opium.

Zarghuna Girls
School in Kabul,
Afghanistan, 2002.
The United
Nations Children's
Fund, or UNICEF,
helped the school
with educational
supplies and teacher
training, and assisted
in repairing the
infrastructure after
the 2001 departure
of the Taliban, which
had turned the
institution for the
education of girls into
a religious school for
boys, from Kabul.

Women in Laos
weeding their rice
fields as part of
integrated agro-
forestry, 2012. The
United Nations
Forum on Forests
promotes the
management,
conservation,
and sustainable
development of
forests.

understanding of the kinds of issues I would come to deal with later on. I saw that idealism and realism are not mutually exclusive, and that it is enormously difficult to achieve lasting results unless the parties to a conflict are sincere in their search for a solution and are prepared to work together for a fair compromise.

Furthermore, genuine commitment from the United Nations is needed if tangible results are being seriously sought. It is very clear to me that had I not had the best possible women and men from the United Nations system, and the Member States, at my service, the successful implementation of the United Nations plan would have been much more difficult. Strong support from Secretary-General Javier Pérez de Cuéllar and my senior colleagues at the United Nations was also of the utmost importance in guaranteeing our success.

In all large United Nations operations, the major powers, first and foremost the five per-manent members of the Security Council, are in a key position. Their support and cooperation are essential. At a minimum it is vital that the solution proposed is acceptable, or at least tolerated, by them. Countries affected by a conflict, because they may host refugees or have other legitimate interests to safeguard, can be a great asset if they choose to cooperate, as the Frontline States did in the case of Namibia.

New Challenges and Opportunities

After a successful United Nations mission in Namibia, it was time to return to New York. Secretary-General de Cuéllar asked me to return to my former position as Under-Secretary-General for Administration and Management, to which I had been appointed in 1987. The challenges were daunting. The financial situation of the United Nations was dire. Budget

cuts, redundancies, reorganization: these were not popular themes. But with the cooperation of the staff they were manageable. The poor financial state was due largely to the unwillingness of some members to pay their dues, as required. It was not easy to convince the United States Congress that it was in the country's interests to share the responsibility of overcoming the financial crisis.

In 1991, I returned to Finland and to the Foreign Ministry, a change for my family as well as for myself. My career had been that of a civil servant—both in the service of my own country and with the United Nations. Most of the time I had either served abroad or worked in foreign affairs. Back at home, it was a tumultuous time in European politics. The collapse of the Soviet Union and the end of the Cold War were changes of monumental proportion for the international community and the United Nations.

It was somewhat of a surprise to me that my service in Namibia and on other United Nations projects had been well noticed in Finland, but that service provided the background to future developments. I was asked to stand for office in the 1994 presidential election. This idea was new to me—I had, after all, never held any political office, nor had I been active in party politics. Nevertheless the party decided to choose me as its candidate in the elections in February of that year. It was soon evident that I had a real chance to be elected, and 1 March 1994 was the day of my presidential inauguration. During my term as President of Finland, the most important development from a national point of view was the successful conclusion of negotiations for membership in the European Union. In other parts of Europe, however, and in the Balkans in particular, there were fewer reasons to celebrate.

Woman standing in a field near Timbuktu, Mali, 2013. Among the tasks of the United Nations Multidimensional Integrated Stabilization Mission in Mali is helping farmers' cooperatives resume rice production after the end of rebel occupation of the area.

The United Nations and the War in the Balkans

The breakup of Yugoslavia was a long, bloody process in which I played several roles. During the Bosnian War, which took place during my tenure as Secretary of State in the Finnish Ministry for Foreign Affairs, I was appointed as the Chairman of the Bosnia and Herzegovina Working Group of the International Conference on the Former Yugoslavia of 1992–1993.

Later, I served as Special Advisor to the United Nations Secretary-General's Special Representative for the former Yugoslavia, Thorvald Stoltenberg. Bosnia and Herzegovina had seen extreme destruction and human loss. The war in Bosnia had been one where the credibility of the United Nations had been challenged. It was important that whenever a comparable crisis emerged, the United Nations would resolve it successfully.

Another flashpoint in the former Yugoslavia was Kosovo. Ethnic Albanians formed the majority of the population in the territory, but the Serbs constituted an important minority. Albanian nationalism was kindled by the cancellation of autonomy. The response was the creation of a resistance movement and reciprocal acts of violence and atrocities. Some 800,000 Albanians were forced out of their homes. All efforts to find a peaceful settlement to the conflict with external help were unsuccessful and led to military intervention by NATO.

A decisive turn, from my viewpoint, occurred in May 1999 when the American and Russian governments asked me to join them in finding an end to the crisis. NATO had been bombing targets in Yugoslavia for some time to put an end to the repression in Kosovo. It was obvious that the rule of President Slobodan Milošević had to come to an end. After United States Deputy Secretary of State Strobe Talbott, former Rus-

sian Prime Minister Viktor Chernomyrdin, and I had come to an understanding of a proposal to be made to President Milošević, Chernomyrdin and I went to Belgrade to meet with him. He understood that he was facing a united front. He accepted the terms offered, and Kosovo was placed under United Nations administration in 1999 by Resolution 1244 of the United Nations Security Council. The crisis took place at a time when relations between European Union members and the United States on the one hand and the Russian Federation on the other were propitious for political cooperation. President Boris Yeltsin of Russia was genuinely interested in showing that he was ready and able to lead his country towards something that in those days was called "the common European home." That was an essential precondition for the success of the Kosovo crisis settlement.

In November 2005, United Nations Secretary-General Kofi Annan asked if I would be prepared to be his representative in Kosovo to facilitate the status process. I accepted, and the work was mainly conducted in Vienna, where the Austrian government provided good facilities for the effort. The task we were faced with was not easy. Results were difficult to achieve. There were, however, indications that Russia would not block Kosovo's independence, but in the end it withdrew its consent, which led to the unilateral declaration of independence by Kosovo in 2008.

Much has been said and written about the Balkans. It has been asserted that the independence of Kosovo was a grave mistake and a breach of international law. However, there is an authoritative response to that claim: the International Court of Justice gave an advisory opinion, to a request put forward by Serbia, on the issue of the legality of Kosovo's declaration of independence. In that opinion the Court found that the declaration of independence did not violate international law.

Working for Peace in a Fragmented World

Often, in internal conflicts, States are not keen on internationalizing their disputes and shy away from visibly involving international organizations in their resolution. In these cases, non-governmental actors can be useful as objective, nimble, behind-the scenes partners that run less of a risk for the conflicting sides.

In 2000, after my term as President of Finland, I established the Crisis Management Initiative, a nonprofit organization focusing on conflict resolution and peacebuilding. This I did not only because of my personal commitment to peace but because it had become clear to me that the changed nature of conflicts in the new century would require new capacities and approaches.

The complicated world of peacemaking became apparent in the question of the political status of the Indonesian province of Aceh. An attempt to establish a ceasefire in Aceh had failed earlier, half a year after it had been agreed upon, and the fighting continued. The tsunami of 26 December 2004 created a new situation. The destruction was enormous and the human toll extreme, which highlighted the urgency of establishing a political solution that would allow the reconstruction process to begin. The Indonesian government was ready to start negotiations towards creating an autonomous province in Aceh; a greater degree of self-government was the basis upon which the talks could be started. That foundation proved to be the agreed way forward, but it still took time and a good deal of exertion to find a mutually acceptable formula for an agreement.

The Aceh negotiations were conducted in Finland, in an isolated manor house, a location helpful in ensuring that unwelcome publicity would be avoided. After only seven months the negotiations were successfully concluded. The process showed me that non-State actors and what is now called Track 2/Track 3 diplomacy—in which official and non-official actors cooperate in conflict resolution—play a pivotal role in solving conflicts and building sustainable peace in the current world of political, cultural, and economic fragmentation.

The United Nations and Multilateral Diplomacy

I have often been asked if a person acting as a mediator in a crisis situation should be neutral. Invariably my answer is that the qualities required for the task are summed up by the phrase "honest broker." A mediator must steer the process through his or her own initiatives and suggestions in order to be an asset to the process. A mediator should be an independent actor, not one who is subject to control by any government or institution. It is only then that such an individual's integrity and honest determination to seek an equitable settlement can be deemed credible.

Crises take many shapes and no two crises are likely to be identical, or even related or comparable. What is crucial is establishing a human relationship with the parties and acting in a manner that convinces them of the sincerity of the mediator. No settlement is possible unless the parties to the conflict desire a solution to their differences. Often negotiations are conducted without the necessary sincerity or good

Nelson Mandela, President of the Republic of South Africa, addressing the fifty-third session of the General Assembly at the United Nations Headquarters in New York, 1998. In 2009, the General Assembly declared his birthday, 18 July, Nelson Mandela International Day in recognition of his service to humanity in the fields of "conflict resolution, race relations, promotion and protection of human rights, reconciliation, gender equality and the rights of children and other vulnerable groups, as well as the upliftment of poor and underdeveloped communities."

Women in El Fasher,
North Darfur, Sudan,
2010. A march for "six
days of activism against
gender-based violence"
marks an annual
campaign beginning
on 25 November, the
International Day to
End Violence Against
Women, and ending on
1 December, Human
Rights Day.

Young girl from Kosovo
at a refugee camp in
Albania, 1999. The Office
of the United Nations
High Commissioner for
Refugees, which was
established in 1951
to help the estimated
1 million people still
uprooted after World
War II to return home,
manages the refugee
camps. At the beginning
of 2013, the number
of refugees in the care
of UNHCR stood at
10.4 million. At the end
of 2012, the UNHCR
was also caring for 15.5
million people displaced
within their own country.
A further 4.8 million
registered refugees are
looked after in some 60
camps in the Middle East
by the United Nations
Relief and Works Agency
for Palestine Refugees in
the Near East, which was
set up in 1949 to care for
displaced Palestinians.

faith. In such circumstances the negotiations turn into a publicity stunt, an effort to make a point and to put the blame on the other party.

I have stated it earlier but it bears repeating: I have learned from my tasks that cooperation with the permanent members of the United Nations Security Council is crucial. In my experience, for the mediator to be successful, the support of the United States government is vital. There are instances when the permanent members of the Security Council abstain from obstructing the process. Benign abstention can also be a silent contribution to the settlement of a difficult issue.

To work under the auspices of the United Nations can be an asset of the greatest value. Only the United Nations can give the needed legitimacy to operations where force cannot be avoided in order to prevent greater evils. In these circumstances, the Secretary-General of the United Nations, together with the perma-

nent members of the Security Council, holds a key position.

While acknowledging the fact that the United Nations is still needed—maybe even more than ever—we have to be frank and forward-looking. Old tools and approaches are not always enough to solve current complex crises. The United Nations has proved its flexibility and willingness to adapt to the changing nature of conflicts, but more needs to be done. Fragile societies and States need support on all possible fronts; while many non-State actors can be beneficial in this work, the United Nations has to be able to do more.

Sometimes internal conflicts cannot be solved because one party or another does not accept those in power, for example to organize legitimate elections. One option may be to mandate and provide resources to the United Nations to organize elections in societies that for conflict or other reasons have lost the ability to do so

for themselves. This might provide more alternatives for solving disputes when the parties cannot agree on how elections can be organized. The United Nations offers expertise in organizing elections. Indeed, strengthening and supporting all possible democratic powers and systems lies at the heart of the Organization.

My years with the United Nations have given me great confidence in the capacity of the Organization to solve problems of war and peace, of strife and conflict. Success cannot always be guaranteed. There are cases where the contribution of the United Nations can come only after other actors have taken the initiative to seek a solution to a problem. But if the United Nations can be engaged in the process so that the solution has the seal of the Organization, then the prospects of success are greatly improved. Our world of multiple, complex crises continues to place great responsibility on the United Nations to live up to its mandate and to adapt to the world as

it looks today. Positive advances have been made with the rapid development of conflict resolution and mediation capacities, as well as in the response to current development challenges.

Striving for Human Rights and Social Justice

It cannot be forgotten that the United Nations is not solely about conflicts and operations. Throughout its history, one of the greatest achievements of the Organization has been its work in contributing to human rights for all and, in a determined way, to sustainable social and economic development. Every day, the United Nations tackles extreme poverty and inequality all over the world and mobilizes action on climate change. Critics of the United Nations tend to easily ignore or forget these efforts.

In setting the Millennium Development Goals—to address the root causes of poverty, to

promote gender equality and empower women, to improve maternal health, to achieve universal primary education, to reduce child mortality, to combat malaria and HIV/AIDS, to ensure environmental sustainability, and to develop a global partnership for development—the United Nations returned to its raison d'être. Although the realities of billions of people are still complex and grim, the average figures are much better than they were before the MDGs were launched in 2000. Much progress has been made, but what worries me is that at the same time injustice and inequality have been increasing, not only globally, but also within national and regional boundaries. Inequality is the most serious challenge of our time, and I have been happy to observe that the United Nations is responding to this in its Post-2015 Development Agenda.

In the seventieth anniversary year of its founding, and as the United Nations constantly aims to improve its effectiveness and ability to react, the old wisdom still carries relevance. The challenges are not only bureaucratic; the questions are not only those of organizational effectiveness. They are also political. The United Nations is as relevant and effective an Organization as the Member States want it to be.

Martti Ahtisaari, former President of the Republic of Finland, has served the United Nations in many capacities. He was a driving force behind the independence of Namibia and the resolution of conflict in the former Yugoslavia, served as Under-Secretary-General for Administration and Management, and as the chair of an independent panel on the security and safety of United Nations personnel in Iraq in 2003, as well as United Nations Special Envoy for the Horn of Africa, 2003–2005. President Ahtisaari's work as Special Envoy for the future status process for Kosovo led to Kosovo's declaration of independence in 2008. He was also instrumental in finding a peaceful solution to the conflict in the Indonesian province of Aceh. President Ahtisaari was awarded the Nobel Peace Prize in 2008.

UNITED NATIONS

Charter of The United Nations

1945

REPRODUCTION of the opening page, giving the text of the preamble, the first five signatures, the last page and the certificate appended to the duplicate copies—of the Charter of the United Nations signed in San Francisco on June 26th, 1945.

Issued by
UNITED NATIONS INFORMATION OFFICE
610 FIFTH AVENUE · NEW YORK 20, N. Y.

LEFT
"Charter of the United Nations" poster. The United Nations Department of Public Information issued this poster in 1950 in the series "Documents of Freedom." The Charter shows the original United Nations logo.

PAGES 38–39
Helicopter bearing Lambert Mende Omalanga, Minister of Communications of the Democratic Republic of the Congo, 2014. Omalanga conducted talks with rebels from the Democratic Forces for the Liberation of Rwanda, who had recently surrendered, at the Kanyabayonga base of the United Nations Organization Stabilization Mission in the Democratic Republic of the Congo.

Rekindling the Dream

CARTER WISEMAN

When most people think about the world's iconic works of architecture, they are likely to consider the pyramids at Giza, the Taj Mahal, and perhaps St. Paul's Cathedral in London. After that, they might add more recent examples, such as New York's 1958 Seagram Building, the 1996 Petronas Towers in Kuala Lumpur, or Burj Khalifa in Dubai, which in 2010 set a record for the world's tallest structure. Impressive as all these buildings may be, they represent some rather traditional areas of architectural activity. Two (the pyramids and the Taj) are memorials to the dead, one (St. Paul's) is a religious shrine, and the remaining three are monuments of commerce. Only one building can claim its place on the list of international architectural landmarks as a symbol of the world's most enduring aspiration: peace.

Completed in 1952, the Headquarters of the United Nations, on the eastern edge of New York City's Manhattan Island, embraces the highest hopes of humanity as no other building does. Conceived in the shadow of the failed League of Nations and the aftermath of World War II, the United Nations complex is the only place on the planet where representatives of all countries are invited to confront their shared concerns and conflicts. While individual agendas may include famine, disease, the environment, or sectarian strife, the overarching text of the United Nations is how to survive as a species.

By the early twenty-first century, however, the survival of the United Nations Headquarters itself had been called into question. After more than 50 years, the green-glass facades of the 39-storey slab of the Secretariat Building, which housed staff offices, were leaking, as was the roof of the General Assembly, where the delegates met for deliberations. The Conference Building, home to three important meeting chambers, had fallen below fire and safety standards, as had the other buildings of the United Nations. Asbestos, once considered an insulating and fire-proofing miracle and existing throughout the complex, had long since been identified as a deadly health hazard. Most troubling, in a world where terrorist attacks were becoming a grim fact of life, security was an increasing concern.

The United Nations faced a formidable choice: should its Headquarters be renovated or replaced? Some speculated that demolishing the original structures and starting over might be more efficient and less expensive than fixing them. In the end, however, the United Nations

decided to renew itself, a decision consequential both symbolically and financially.

Well before the end of World War II, the Allied leaders had started to plan an international organization intended to prevent future global conflicts. Mindful of the fate of the League of Nations, they ensured that the location of any new headquarters would be agreed to by all parties. The first meeting of the General Assembly, which took place in London, settled on the United States as the host; proposals for the actual site ranged from San Francisco to Philadelphia to Boston. Among the candidates was New York City's Flushing Meadows, which had languished unused since the 1939 World's Fair, and Connecticut's Fairfield County.

By happy coincidence, in the autumn of 1946, just as the United Nations was prospecting for a home, the legendary New York City real estate developer William Zeckendorf was formulating plans for what he called X City, a massive mixed-use complex he hoped would rival Rockefeller Center. Zeckendorf had assembled a site, an expanse of slaughterhouses and tenements abutting the East River north of Forty-second Street, and had gone so far as to select an architect, Wallace Harrison, who had worked on Rockefeller Center and the main buildings of the 1939 World's Fair. But Zeckendorf had not been able to put enough money together to close the deal. At the same time, the Rockefeller family was trying to attract the United Nations to New York by offering a better site than those that had been put forward.

Through the initiative of Nelson Rockefeller, and with the financial commitment of his father, John D. Rockefeller Jr., Harrison spearheaded an arrangement whereby Zeckendorf would sell the parcel to the United Nations for $8.5 million, his asking price; the Rockefellers would write the check. On the morning of 11 December 1946, this proposal was brought to the attention of the Headquarters Committee by the United States delegation; by that afternoon, the committee members were on a site visit. Shortly thereafter, the group agreed to recommend the acceptance of the Rockefeller gift, securing the East Midtown site as the location for the permanent headquarters.

Once the site and financial gift were agreed to by the General Assembly, the next step was

to assemble a design team. The United Nations' first Secretary-General, Trygve Lie, former Foreign Minister of Norway, created a Board of Design and appointed his new friend Harrison to direct it based largely on Harrison's work at Rockefeller Center and the World's Fair. Harrison's responsibility as Director of Planning included overseeing the contributions of the other architects selected for the team: the Swiss-French Le Corbusier, Oscar Niemeyer from Brazil, Sweden's Sven Markelius, Nikolai D. Bassov of the USSR, Gaston Brunfaut of Belgium, Canada's Ernest Cormier, Howard Robertson of the United Kingdom, Ssu-Ch'eng Liang from China, Australia's Gyle A. Soilleux, and Julio Vilamajó of Uruguay. (Several obvious candidates were excluded based on the makeup of the United Nations at the time. Alvar Aalto's native Finland was not yet a member of the organization, and Ludwig Mies van der Rohe and Walter Gropius had links to Germany, also not yet a Member State.)

Le Corbusier was clearly the most prominent of the group. He had been a pioneer of European modernism and in 1927 had competed (unsuccessfully) for the design of the League of Nations Headquarters in Geneva. The fundamental forms of the buildings as eventually constructed were Le Corbusier's and Niemeyer's. Le Corbusier suggested that the facades of the Secretariat be clad in brise-soleils, his signature concrete sunshades; fortunately, the proposition was rejected for an environment where ice was a consideration. Instead, the building became the first in New York to have all-glass curtain walls.

A less successful alteration to the initial scheme was the addition of a dome to the roof of the General Assembly Building. Vermont's former Senator Warren Austin, the Permanent Representative of the United States to the United Nations, had insisted on a dome in order to persuade Congress to provide the United States share of the construction cost: he argued that no ceremonial building in America should be without one. As built, the slender Secretariat rose 544 feet into the Manhattan sky and measured a mere 72 feet in width. The General Assembly was linked to the Secretariat by the lower mass of the Conference Building, both of which are traditionally attributed to Niemeyer. Construction began in 1949 and was completed in 1952.

The building made the cover of *Life* magazine on 3 November 1952. The public seemed to accept with enthusiasm the addition to New York City's spicy architectural stew. However, as is so often the case, the views of the cultural sophisticates diverged, and the reaction to the complex among some leading commentators was surprisingly negative. The famously contrarian architect Frank Lloyd Wright condemned the Secretariat as "a deadpan box with no expression of the nature of what transpires in the building." Lewis Mumford, architecture critic for the *New Yorker*, found the ensemble "a blending of the grandiose and the obvious" and slammed the Secretariat as "a superficial aesthetic triumph and an architectural failure." In *Architectural Forum*, Paul Rudolph, who would later design some of the country's most uninhabitable concrete buildings, damned the interiors

of the General Assembly Building for bringing "the so-called International Style close to bankruptcy" and declared the entire complex "a background for a grade 'B' movie about 'one world.'" The outcome was not unlike the reception that had greeted Rockefeller Center, also censured at its birth by many of the intellectual elite.

In the years that followed, the building fell victim to deferred maintenance. Funds that might have gone into routine repairs were put off for essential programs. (One ambassador had to sit through a meeting with an umbrella over his head.) Although it became clear that the campus had to be renewed, the idea did not sit well in certain circles, especially among some of the Member States that would have to bear the heaviest cost.

Such opposition was eventually overcome, and planning for the renovation began in 2000. In 2003, the Capital Master Plan was launched, and in 2007, Michael Adlerstein, the former Chief Historic Architect for the United States National Park Service, was appointed Executive Director. Adlerstein trained as an architect at the Rensselaer Polytechnic Institute and at Harvard's Graduate School of Design, where he was a Loeb Fellow. His previous restoration work included Ellis Island, the Statue of Liberty, and other American icons.

Adlerstein's mission was clear, but daunting. "There was a brief discussion about demolition as an option, but the respect for our heritage in the committees of the General Assembly was powerful," Adlerstein said. "Selecting me with my preservation and sustainability background made the institution's direction clear." Adlerstein received strong endorsement from Secretary-General Ban Ki-moon, who appointed him an Assistant Secretary-General with authority over all renovation and restoration matters.

The decision to restore the United Nations rather than demolish or update it was not as simple as it might have seemed. There is a tendency in architecture to succumb to a variation on the Oedipus complex—attacking one's parents while embracing one's grandparents. Rockefeller Center, the Chrysler Building, the Empire State, and countless other works of architecture were denounced by the leading critics of their day only to be celebrated by later generations. It was not until 1963, after the destruction of McKim, Mead & White's majestic neo-Roman Pennsylvania Station of 1910, that New York City established a law to protect architectural landmarks, a statute that became a model for the rest of the country. But even today, Americans are generally more comfortable with landmarks that have been blessed by time: brick, clapboard, and limestone tend to trump glass, steel, and concrete. Corporate modernism, of which the United Nations is a prime example, is not universally chic. "Most people may not love the 1950s yet," said Adlerstein, "but this building is beloved."

The team went through some early turmoil, but the main players were soon in place, including experts in architectural design, engineering, curtain-wall construction, and other technical specialties. The cost of the work was estimated at almost $2 billion, which was secured by an

The Secretariat Building rising from the Headquarters construction site, 1950–51.

assessment on all Member States. Initially, the Japanese architect Fumihiko Maki was to build a 35-storey administrative building in a city park to the south of the Secretariat to house United Nations meetings and staff offices during construction. After renovations were complete, the building would have been used to consolidate United Nations functions that had overflowed into the surrounding city. The plan, however, was put on indefinite hold due to issues involving city-owned property. Instead, a temporary structure on the United Nations' North Lawn housed conferencing functions, and office functions were relocated to rented space elsewhere. The Dag Hammarskjöld Library at the south end of the campus, named for the United Nations' second Secretary-General, was originally included in the renovation. But the four-storey building is considered too structurally fragile to be brought up to current security standards, and its future remains unclear.

In light of the United Nations' history of diligently following protocol, some staff assumed that the restoration project would die a bureaucratic death; the relocation to temporary quarters was something of a culture shock. And when the staff returned to the renovated premises, they faced a new reality: the leadership of every United Nations office was housed in the Secretariat, not just the departments that were created in 1952. The new office space was open, colourful, and sustainable, with views from river to river and shared lighting, air conditioning, and infrastructure. Many traditionalists were annoyed at the loss of their former "high-wall"

private offices; but the new arrangement, in which senior officials were no longer scattered in rental buildings, generated a new level of collegiality. As Susan Kibue, a member of the project's Advisory Board from Kenya, observed, "Generally, all the new spaces had improved natural lighting and better interiors with good colour and lighting design that also improved the quality of the working environment."

Other obstacles arose. One proposal recommended relocating the in-house printing facilities to make room for other space demands. But, said K. T. Ravindran, an Advisory Board architect from India, "It was important to keep the objectives simple. The CMP's mandate was to make the campus modern, safe, secure, sustainable, and accessible, while respecting the architectural integrity of the original design." In respect to this mandate, Brazilian Advisory Board member Jayme Zettel, who as a young designer had worked in the office of the late Oscar Niemeyer, praised the "excellency of the work done during the restoration process [which] kept the modern characteristics of the buildings." One aspect of the original Headquarters that did not need significant alteration was the distribution of the buildings' functions. "The systems were old and tired," said Susan Kibue, "but the CMP started out with a building complex that functioned well as a first-class conference centre."

Many visitors to the United Nations' 18-acre complex are unaware that they are on sovereign territory. The United Nations is not obligated to comply with local laws and codes. However, the organization is dependent on New York City

emergency services in the event of a crisis, so the restoration team honoured local fire and safety codes. But doing so added to the complexity of the repairs. Concrete floor slabs had deteriorated and had to be reinforced with steel. According to Robert Heintges, an expert on glass curtain walls, the facades of the Secretariat were "a disaster in terms of leaks." The leaks included water, which penetrated the work spaces, and air, which flowed out of the building with such force that in the winter snow was pushed upward. To establish the colour of the original glass panels, which over the years had been coated with plastic film to reduce glare, Heintges had to work from a sample of the 1952 glass discovered in the archives. Some of the metal frames were in danger of falling, so all 5,040 single-glazed panes were replaced, but not before a mock-up was built on the front lawn. "It was an incredible responsibility," said Heintges. "No failure allowed."

Restoring the glass addressed the major problems with the exterior, but scores of others lurked inside. Drainage pipes that had been run into the building were flooding staff offices. The heating and air conditioning systems were obsolete, and the volume of asbestos was "overwhelming," according to Adlerstein. Decades of tobacco smoke had given much of the building a brown patina. (The original design had called for ashtrays in the men's toilets large enough to accommodate cigars.) The United Nations estimates that it is saving 50 per cent on its electrical use (much of the new lighting is LED) and consumes 40 per cent less water. The renovation was also a major boost for the makers of Naugahyde,

a plastic substitute for leather: the seats in the meeting rooms were reupholstered in their original 1950s shades of rust and turquoise.

In more tranquil times, tending to such issues might have been routine, but in today's world, security looms over any major architectural project, especially one that involves representatives of every nation in the world. All the glass, including the revolving doors, had to be made blast-resistant. Part of the original Conference Building was cantilevered over the FDR Drive along the East River, in danger of possible attack by a truck bomb from below. Consequently, several meeting rooms were moved away from the overhang, which involved additional concrete and steel reinforcement and set the project's calendar back by a year. (Though an unexpected benefit of the relocation was the addition of a large lounge with river views inserted where the conference rooms had been.) The United States—under the terms of its agreement with the United Nations to provide security as host nation—contributed $100 million to cover the cost in addition to the United Nations–wide assessment.

While the international aesthetic of the 1950s drove most of the interior renovations, a regional component is evident in the restoration of the Conference Building. The project management team was especially interested in the three large chambers that had been designed in the Scandinavian style with financial support from Denmark, Norway, and Sweden. (All three nations voluntarily contributed additional funds

Original air conditioning control panels in the chiller plant in the basement. After more than 60 years, the building systems had far exceeded their service life.

to the restoration project for this effort.) One problem was replacing the carpet in the Trusteeship Council Chamber, which had long since been worn through and removed. The team worked from a 1950s photograph showing the then King of Morocco standing on the original. By estimating his shoe size at nine or ten, the designers extrapolated the dimensions of the carpet motif and had a replica made.

One concern the United Nations may actually welcome is the future of its art collection. Over the years, many countries have donated valuable works by their own artists to the institution, including the murals *War* and *Peace*, by the Brazilian artist Cândido Portinari, and *Brotherhood*, by the Mexican artist Rufino Tamayo. When the renovation was announced, many of the works were sent home to be cleaned and restored. In almost every case, their value has increased since they were donated, so the United Nations now has a security problem of another, happier, kind.

The General Assembly Building, the last building to be renovated, was reopened on 15 September 2014, just in time to host the sixty-ninth session of the General Assembly. The event provoked widespread media coverage, some of which returned to a question that has dogged the United Nations since its creation: how influential is the institution in a world seemingly condemned to a permanent state of crisis? In fact, the United Nations seems more relevant than ever: climate change, the health threats of AIDS and Ebola, and the rise of militant religious extremism are not matters limited to national borders. Indeed, the problems faced by the international community are now less international than supranational; they are no longer bound by relations among countries with borders, flags, and anthems. The United Nations' membership has grown from 51 members in 1947 to 193 in 2015. The building now accommodates 8,000 meetings a year, and the renovation has provided seating for the present membership (with modest space for growth).

Whatever its limitations, the United Nations remains a shrine to hope. Its renewal has had a spiritual dimension as well as a physical one. Even if some of its original critics may not have ranked the original design among

LEFT

The Conference Building under renovation. In 2010, after a series of terrorist attacks on United Nations facilities, the United Nations increased requirements for blast protection at the Headquarters compound. Structural changes to the building and security enhancements within delayed the completion of the Conference Building by a year.

ABOVE

Deputy Secretary-General Jan Eliasson, Assistant Secretary-General Michael Adlerstein, and Secretary-General Ban Ki-moon in the General Assembly Hall during the renovation.

the most aesthetically refined, altering it now would compromise the goal of honouring the institution as it was when its ideals were framed. For a critical period in the 1940s and 1950s, collegiality overruled individuality. So it should some 70 years later. No advocate of parliamentary democracy would suggest modernizing the Houses of Parliament any more than a twenty-first-century Catholic would propose updating St. Peter's in Rome. According to the people closest to the project, the reaction of the members has been positive. "There is tremendous affection and emotional investment in this place," said Kent Barwick, who served as chair of the Capital Master Plan Advisory Board. "All the Member States recognized that." A measure of that conclusion is that all the Member States paid their full share of the renovation cost, regardless of how they felt about each other politically.

In his 1994 account of the meetings on the design of the United Nations complex, George Dudley, an architect and associate of Wallace Harrison's, noted that in 1946 his boss had framed the goals of the building in elegantly simple terms: "The basic problem is not to try to symbolize the United Nations in some highly imaginative design, but to construct a Capitol where the world representatives can work efficiently and in comfort." Those goals may seem modest for such a globally ambitious undertaking. But they can also be seen as appropriate for an organization in which individual needs and wants have been, since its founding, balanced with the greater good. Now that efficiency and comfort

have been restored—and secured—the pursuit of the greater good can go forward afresh.

The United Nations Headquarters buildings are not the pyramids, but the pharaohs who built those monuments to themselves are long gone. Religion is not what it was when Christopher Wren designed St. Paul's and the Church of England ruled much of the world, as well as the waves. At some point, a building will rise higher than Burj Khalifa. Yet the United Nations, if cared for, may prevail as the one place where humanity's great questions are negotiated peacefully.

Reflecting on the seven-year saga of renewing the campus, Secretary-General Ban Ki-moon took a broad view. At the ceremony marking the completion of the Secretariat Building renovation, he said: "Let us marvel at the renewal of this landmark. Every day, thousands of staff, delegates and visitors pass through these halls. Every day, we seek to advance the cause of peace, development and justice. Today begins a new era in the vital work of service to the world's people."

———

Carter Wiseman is the author of Twentieth-Century American Architecture: The Buildings and Their Makers, *as well as biographies of I. M. Pei and Louis Kahn. A graduate of Yale College, he earned a master's degree in architectural history at Columbia University and was a Loeb Fellow in Advanced Environmental Studies at Harvard University's Graduate School of Design. He is the former President of the MacDowell Colony, the nation's oldest retreat for creative artists.*

United Nations Capital Master Plan

The United Nations Headquarters in 2015, after renovation under the Capital Master Plan. The Secretariat (centre), General Assembly (foreground), and Conference (left) Buildings were gutted and refurbished almost in their entirety. Both the activities and the staff of the United Nations were relocated during the construction. A temporary building provided accommodation for conference functions, and the Security Council moved to an interim chamber in the General Assembly Building. More than 6,000 employees were transferred to temporary quarters.

Secretariat Building

The Secretariat Building stands as the defining icon of the United Nations Headquarters. Heavily influenced by the architectural vision of Le Corbusier, and constructed from 1949 to 1950, the sleek, 39-storey tower is distinguished by its non-structural glass facade, the first curtain wall built on such a massive scale. Since its completion, the Secretariat has become a prototype of the modern office building. The staff of the United Nations Secretariat moved into the building in 1951; by the next year, more than 3,000 employees occupied the building. The Secretary-General and his staff reside on the thirty-eighth floor.

The Secretariat Building was emptied in advance of its restoration, which began in 2010; all staff relocated to rented office space or to a temporary building on the North Lawn. The first phase of the renovation involved the abatement of all asbestos-containing materials; demolition down to the bare concrete slabs followed. The most noticeable aspect of the renovation of the Secretariat was the replacement of the curtain wall, which had become leaky and structurally unstable. Also, the transparency and greyish-blue hue of the original glazing had been compromised by the application of insulation and blast-protection coatings. Thanks to extensive tests, the building now replicates its appearance in 1951.

In 2007, Secretary-General Ban Ki-moon envisioned the renovated United Nations compound as a "globally acclaimed model of efficient use of energy and resources." In fact, the energy consumption of the entire compound has been halved. Among the measures installed in the Secretariat, in addition to the new double-glazed curtain wall (the initial version was only single-glazed), are more efficient air conditioning equipment, high-tech temperature control systems, and automated blinds in all windows.

The interior of the tower was updated to create a less hierarchical and more sustainable workplace for the twenty-first century. Before the renovation, offices in the Secretariat were enclosed by floor-to-ceiling walls and doors. Most of the staff members who moved back to the renovated building in 2012 and 2013 work in open stations, and various informal meeting spaces foster teamwork. The office floors are suffused with natural light, and the glorious views east and west are enjoyed by all building occupants. The open office environment also reduces energy consumption, as do features like a daylight-harvesting system, making for a greener United Nations.

The Secretariat Building post-renovation.

LEFT
The Secretariat towering over the dome of the General Assembly, 1951. Construction of the compound was almost completed.

OPPOSITE
The Conference, Secretariat, and General Assembly Buildings from the North Lawn, 1954.

The lobby of the
Secretariat Building
from the south, 1951.

OPPOSITE
The Secretariat under renovation. A construction hoist on the east facade of the building hauled construction material and debris. In the course of the construction work, 95 per cent of all construction waste was diverted from landfills and recycled.

RIGHT
Replacement of the curtain wall. The complete renewal of the building envelopes, especially the glazed facades of the Secretariat Building, was a critical and highly visible step in reducing overall energy consumption by at least 50 per cent, with energy use for heating and air conditioning lowered by 65 per cent. In addition, greenhouse gas emissions were decreased by 45 per cent.

PAGES 74–75
Curtain wall replacement. Only a few glass panels remain to be installed on the east facade.

PAGES 76–77
The west facade of the Secretariat after renovation. Although the new curtain wall is indistinguishable from the original—the first constructed at such a large scale—it performs much better in terms of energy efficiency and blast protection.

PAGES 78–79
The lighted lobby of the Secretariat Building from the Secretary-General's entrance. A symphony in marble and glass, this entry is reserved for dignitaries.

LEFT AND OPPOSITE
Sunset and evening views of the Secretariat. Transparency, one of the guiding principles of the United Nations Headquarters design, is once again evident on the renovated facade.

Secretariat roof during renovation. The roof served as a staging area where derricks raised and lowered multi-storey work platforms for the demolition of the old curtain wall and the installation of the new one.

RIGHT AND OPPOSITE
Demolition underway within the Secretariat Building. Only the bare concrete slabs were preserved. The United Nations Headquarters, although on international territory, was designed to comply with the New York City Building Code of 1938. Over the decades, the buildings fell out of step with changes in the code. With the renovation the compound has been updated to meet current New York City building and life safety codes.

The staff entrance to the Secretariat Building. Three thousand employees work in its offices.

The lobby of the
Secretariat from the
south. The polished
terrazzo floor
reflects portraits
of the former
Secretaries-General.

ABOVE AND RIGHT
New meeting rooms in
the Secretariat Building.
Gathering spaces, now
situated on two floors,
are reserved via a
central system.

Secretariat office floor. Before the renovation, the occupants of the Secretariat Building reflected the United Nations of the 1950s. Departments in existence at the time were accommodated in the tower; those established later had offices outside the compound and were sometimes scattered over many buildings. Now there is office space for the leadership and a number of staff from every department.

Offices in the Secretariat Building. Open plans foster a setting that is more collaborative but still provides a certain level of privacy. Before the renovation, 80 per cent of employees in the Secretariat had private offices, and 20 per cent worked in open stations. The renovation reversed this ratio while offering greater natural light and views.

Informal gathering space
on the twenty-seventh
floor of the Secretariat,
one of two floors
devoted to meeting
rooms. Much of the
existing loose furniture
remains in use.

LEFT
The historic United Nations emblem adorning an elevator cab. The refurbished elevators in the Secretariat Building can reach a maximum speed of 1,200 feet per minute.

OPPOSITE
Corridor leading to the office of the Secretary-General on the thirty-eighth floor of the Secretariat.

PAGES 98–101
The Secretary-General's wood-panelled meeting room.

PAGES 102–3
Flags of all 193 Member States of the United Nations. The colourful array greets delegates on the second floor of the "neck," the junction between the General Assembly and Conference Buildings.

General Assembly Building

The General Assembly brings together visitors and delegates to the United Nations Headquarters. Tourists and other guests to the United Nations enter the Visitors' Lobby, walking across a generous outdoor podium and through an imposing set of bronze doors donated by Canada. The entry area was designed to impress, with boldly curved balconies rising up to the fourth floor, exposed ductwork on the ceiling, and gold-leafed columns that conceal ventilation shafts. Thanks to simple architectural manoeuvres, the entrance lobby appears higher and longer than it is.

United Nations delegates have an entrance of their own, designed to accept automobiles, facing First Avenue. Enhancing the light-flooded Delegates' Lobby is the monumental mural *War* by the Brazilian artist Cândido Portinari, a forceful reminder of the United Nations' determination "to save succeeding generations from the scourge of war," as stated in the preamble to the Charter of the United Nations. The Delegates' Lobby leads to both the grand Plenary Hall of the General Assembly and, through a gallery with the flags of all 193 Member States, to the Conference Building. As they leave the General Assembly, delegates look to Portinari's mural *Peace*, which shows them the joys of a peaceful world.

The renovation of the General Assembly Building in 2013 and 2014 was the last chapter of the Capital Master Plan. The work was completed in 16 months, and the building, which also houses eight conference rooms on the lower level of the basement, was reopened on 15 September 2014, in time to host the closing ceremony of the sixty-eighth session of the General Assembly. The guiding principle was restoration of the original design, generally ascribed to Oscar Niemeyer. Features lost to time, like the colour of the dome on top of the curved roof of the building, were revived. Painted a dull brown in a futile attempt to stop water from dripping into the Plenary Hall, the dome now shines silver once again.

Included in the restoration of the General Assembly Building, and indeed the entire compound, was an upgrade of the electronics infrastructure. The world's business can now be seen and heard around the world. As for the Plenary Hall, it was designed to accommodate a future increase in membership. As the years since 1945 have shown, this is a room where every country wants a seat at the table.

The United Nations Headquarters compound in fall 2014, toward the end of its renovation. During construction work in the General Assembly Building (centre), the General Assembly met in the temporary North Lawn Building (lower left corner). The august body returned to its home in September 2014.

The north facade of the General Assembly Building and the Visitors' Terrace, 1952.

The escalators in the Delegates' Lobby of the General Assembly Building, 1952. This entrance is reserved for delegates.

LEFT
The Visitors' Lobby
at the north of the
General Assembly, 1952.
The imposing space
serves as the starting
point for guided tours
of the United Nations
Headquarters.

PAGES 112–13
The dome of the
General Assembly
Building. New terne-
coated copper cladding
has restored the dome
to its original gleaming
appearance. In the 1950s,
it had been covered with
a thick layer of brownish
paint to keep water
from leaking into the
Plenary Hall.

ABOVE
The new North Screening Building. This structure and its companion to the south have contributed to upgraded security for the United Nations compound. These modest buildings are the first permanent additions to the Headquarters since the 1970s.

OPPOSITE
Sphere within a Sphere by Arnaldo Pomodoro on the Visitors' Terrace. Reflected in the sculpture, a gift from Italy, is the North Screening Building under construction.

ABOVE
Carl Fredrik
Reuterswärd's bronze
sculpture *Non-Violence*.
The work, donated by
Luxembourg, depicts
a revolver with its
barrel tied in a knot.
It is one of the most
photographed pieces
of art at the United
Nations Headquarters.

RIGHT
The equestrian statue
Peace by Antun
Augustinčić, a gift from
Yugoslavia in 1954. The
work was removed
from its pedestal in
early 2008 to make
room for the North
Lawn Building.

PAGES 118–19
The General Assembly
Building from the
south after renovation.
Visible inside the
lighted Delegates'
Lobby are Cândido
Portinari's mural *Peace*,
a gift of Brazil, and
Peter Colfs's tapestry
Triumph of Peace, a gift

of Belgium. A three-
storey "neck" (far
right) connects the
General Assembly
Building and the
Conference Building.

LEFT AND OPPOSITE
The Visitors' Lobby of the General Assembly Building during renovation. A flight of stairs leads down to the Visitors' Concourse.

BOTTOM LEFT
The Delegates' Lobby during the construction work. The escalators that convey delegates from the first floor to the second floor of the General Assembly were rebuilt to their original 1950s look.

OPPOSITE
The Visitors' Lobby post-renovation. The room is as modern in 2014 as it was in 1952, when the building first opened its doors to visitors.

RIGHT
Restored signage above the information counter in the Visitors' Lobby.

OPPOSITE
Uppermost balcony in the
Visitors' Lobby. The three
tiers look down to the public
area and up to the exposed
ductwork on the ceiling.

RIGHT
A graceful steel arch
supporting a walkway in the
Visitors' Lobby.

PAGES 126–27
Visitors' Lobby
with information
counter. The lobby
appears longer than
it is because of slight
inclines up in the
floor and down in
the ceiling toward the
south end of the space.

LEFT
The Visitors' Lobby in
the General Assembly
Building. The portraits
of the Secretaries-
General, woven into
silk carpets as a gift
from Iran, are a popular
photo opportunity.

PAGES 130–31
The Visitors' Lobby in
the General Assembly
Building. The original
design of this area
specified vertical
lighting fixtures inserted
into the columns.
New LED lighting is
equally dramatic and
faithful to the designers'
intentions yet far easier
to maintain.

PAGES 132–33
Scaffolding in the Plenary Hall.

ABOVE
Abstract mural by the French painter Fernand Léger in the Plenary Hall. Another Léger work fills the east wall of the chamber.

OPPOSITE
The floor of the Plenary Hall during renovation work.

PAGES 136–37
Meeting in the Plenary Hall, September 2014. Originally designed when the United Nations had only 51 Member States, the compound was built to accommodate delegates from 70 to 80 countries. By 2014, the number of Member States had grown to 193.

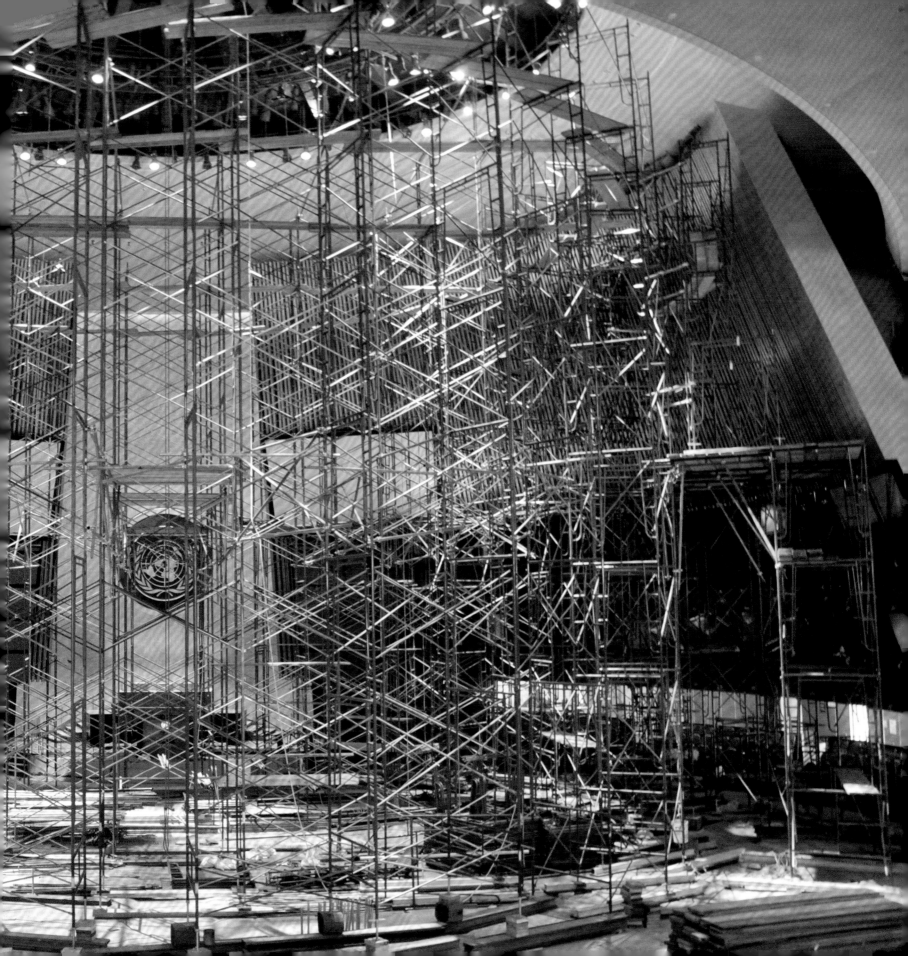

Delegates' seating in the Plenary Hall. At the establishment of the United Nations, each Member State had ten delegates. The General Assembly eventually reduced the number to six in order to accommodate the growing number of Member States. The chairs are upholstered with beige and blue Naugahyde, an artificial leather; leather was considered unfashionable when the Headquarters was designed. Green leather was used on the desks, however.

The inside of the dome of the General Assembly Building, as seen from the floor of the Plenary Hall.

Plenary Hall in summer 2014, three months before reopening. The General Assembly, after considering various scopes and renovation strategies, authorized the Capital Master Plan in 2006 and also approved a special assessment to cover the $1.876 billion budget. In 2007 the delegates approved an accelerated strategy, which required fewer phases of work but more swing spaces for the employees.

ABOVE
Third-floor corridor in the renovated General Assembly Building. Great care was taken to re-create the original colour schemes.

RIGHT
Room GA200, behind the podium of the Plenary Hall. This "green room" offers a moment of quiet to speakers preparing to address the General Assembly before they are escorted to the podium by a protocol officer. The suite, a gift from Switzerland, is also used for meetings between the President of the General Assembly or the Secretary-General and dignitaries.

Conference Building

The Conference Building, less visible than the General Assembly or the Secretariat, is home to three principal bodies of the United Nations: the Security Council, the Economic and Social Council, and the Trusteeship Council. Each council chamber faces the rising sun over the East River. The building itself, boldly cantilevered over the FDR Drive, was designed by the talented structural engineer Nikolai D. Bassov of the Soviet Union.

In addition to the three main chambers, the Conference Building is home to six conference rooms, which host many of the 8,000 meetings that take place at the United Nations Headquarters each year. In addition, the Conference Building provides settings for casual gatherings: the airy North Delegates' Lounge on the second floor, the Delegates' Dining Room on the fourth floor, and the new East Lounge on the first floor, all enhanced by soothing views of the East River, invite delegates to enjoy each other's company and to continue their work informally.

Since the earliest days of the United Nations, the Member States have left their architectural marks within the Conference Building. Restoration of these unique spaces was a paramount consideration during the renovation of the building, which took place between 2010 and 2013. Supported by voluntary contributions, architects and designers selected by the participating Member States worked closely with the Capital Master Plan team to restore some rooms (the three council chambers) and redesign others (the North and South Delegates' Lounges, the East Lounge, and the Security Council Consultation Room and nearby Quiet Room). The rich dialogue between national design visions and classic International Style structure is a distinctive feature of the Conference Building.

Like the entire compound, the Conference Building was designed at a time before terrorism had to be taken into consideration by architects. The renovation of the building required extensive structural enhancements to protect the delegates, staff, and visitors who enter the building each day, participating in and observing international diplomacy in action. Although the celebrated art, furniture, and tapestries donated by Member States may be the most prominent features of the restored Conference Building, the more functional, secure, and comfortable environment enjoyed by the delegates is perhaps the most essential.

View from the
Secretariat Building lobby
to the south facade of
the Conference Building,
1952.

Mosaic of Norman Rockwell's *Golden Rule* in the Conference Building. Guided tours of the United Nations Headquarters, of great value in sharing with visitors the work of the United Nations, continued during the renovation, although the route was abbreviated.

PAGES 150–51 AND RIGHT Hallways in the Conference Building. The United Nations owns an important collection of art, with most works donated by Member States.

Trusteeship Council Chamber

ABOVE
Trusteeship Council
Chamber, 1952.

RIGHT
Trusteeship Council
Chamber, 1977. The
room was remodelled in
1964 to accommodate
the growing number of
Member States. In 1977,
theatre-style seating
for the delegates was
installed. The Capital
Master Plan oversaw
the third renovation
of this chamber.

Hazy view from the
Trusteeship Council
Chamber to the
East River and Long
Island City during
renovation. While
all council chambers
in the Conference
Building have huge
windows, the curtains
are always drawn
since direct sunlight
makes it difficult
to videotape the
meetings.

PAGES 158–61
The Trusteeship
Council Chamber
post-renovation.
The chamber, a gift
from Denmark, was
originally conceived by
Danish architect and
furniture designer Finn
Juhl. The restoration,
supported by a
Danish donation,
returned the
room to a seating
arrangement—flat
floor with concentric
circles—that
respected Juhl's
design intent. New
delegates' tables and
tables and chairs for
the staff servicing
the meetings were
designed by Kasper
Salto and Thomas
Sigsgaard, winners of
a design competition
sponsored by
Denmark.

Mankind and Hope
by Danish sculptor
Henrik Starcke in the
Trusteeship Council
Chamber. Restoration
returned to the work
its original colours, all
but forgotten. Starcke's
figure presides over a
room that has seen its
mission—promoting
development of United
Nations Trust Territories
toward self-government
or independence—
fulfilled. The Council
suspended operations
on 1 November 1994,
after Palau gained
independence. The
Trusteeship Council
Chamber today is
used primarily by the
General Assembly and
its committees.

Concentric circles of seats and desks in the Trusteeship Council Chamber. The colourful boxes on the ceiling, which accommodate light and ventilation, symbolize flags.

Teak-veneered stairs sweeping from balcony to floor in the Trusteeship Council Chamber.

Security Council Chamber

OPPOSITE AND LEFT
Security Council
Chamber, mid-1950s.
The Security Council,
a principal organ of the
United Nations, has
primary responsibility for
maintaining international
peace and security. The
prominent group has
fifteen members, five
permanent ones (China,
France, the Russian
Federation, the United
Kingdom of Great Britain
and Northern Ireland, and
the United States) and
ten non-permanent ones,
each elected for a two-
year term by the General
Assembly. The Security
Council also recommends
to the General Assembly
the appointment of
the Secretary-General
and the admission of
new Member States.
Together with the
General Assembly, it
elects judges to the
International Court
of Justice.

LEFT
Re-installation of Norwegian painter Per Krohg's restored mural *Phoenix Rising from the Ashes* in the Security Council Chamber.

BOTTOM LEFT
Restoration of the textile wall-covering in the Security Council Chamber. Both the original and the modern replica were donated by Norway.

RIGHT
The Security Council Chamber during construction, with padding material for the walls stored in the semicircle of the Security Council table.

PAGES 170–71
The Security Council Chamber post-renovation. A gift from Norway, the room was designed by the Norwegian architect Arnstein Arneberg.

LEFT
Wall-covering in the Security Council Chamber. The motif depicts the anchor of faith, the wheat of hope, and the heart of charity.

BOTTOM LEFT
Inlaid-ash doors to the Security Council Chamber.

OPPOSITE
Krohg's *Phoenix Rising from the Ashes* on the east wall of the Security Council Chamber.

ABOVE
Security Council
Consultation Room.
This meeting space,
redesigned by the
Russian architect
Alexander Konov, is
located in the Security
Council Suite, across
from the Security
Council Chamber. It
was renovated with

a donation from the
Russian Federation.

RIGHT
View of the Security
Council Chamber
from the seat of the
President of the Council.
The presidency rotates
monthly among its fifteen
members.

Economic and Social Council Chamber

Economic and Social
Council Chamber, 1952.
Designed by the Swedish
architect Sven Markelius, it
was a gift from Sweden.

RIGHT
Economic and Social Council, or ECOSOC, Chamber under renovation. All glass facades of the Conference Building were replaced with more sustainable glass.

PAGES 180–81
ECOSOC Chamber post-renovation. Sweden donated a new curtain, *Dialogos*, by Swedish designer Ann Edholm. The Council, one of the principal organs of the United Nations, is the main body for social and environmental issues, as well as for implementation of internationally agreed development goals.

LEFT AND OPPOSITE
ECOSOC Chamber
after restoration, with
refurbished wood tables
and wall battens.

TAPESTRY AFTER GUERNICA
PABLO PICASSO

A LOAN BY MRS. NELSON A. ROCKEFELLER
2015

IN MEMORY OF NELSON A. ROCKEFELLER
AND OF HIS FAITH AND SUPPORT FOR
THE UNITED NATIONS

WOVEN BY
THE ATELIER J. DE LA BAUME DÜRRBACH

North Delegates' Lounge

North Delegates' Lounge, 1976.

ABOVE
Re-installation of *The Great Wall of China* in the North Delegates' Lounge. A gift from China, the tapestry weighs more than 600 pounds and has over 5 million knots.

RIGHT
North Delegates' Lounge under renovation. Long Island City is visible across the East River through a new curtain of porcelain balls created by Dutch designer Hella Jongerius.

PAGES 192–93
North Delegates' Lounge
post-renovation. Sponsored
by a donation from the
Netherlands, the room was
redesigned by Jongerius with
Rem Koolhaas, Irma Boom,
Gabriel Lester, and Louise
Schouwenberg.

LEFT
Original lamps in the
renovated North Delegates'
Lounge.

OPPOSITE
Porcelain balls in the
lounge's new curtain.

RIGHT
South Delegates' Lounge.
The casual meeting
area, donated by Turkey,
provides a quiet space for
delegates near the Security
Council press "stakeout"
area.

PAGES 198–99
Ben Enwonwu's sculpture
Anyanwu in a corridor
near the council chambers.
More than six feet tall, the
work depicts a woman
clad in the regalia of the
ancient kingdom of Royal
Benin, now part of Nigeria.
The piece, a gift from
Nigeria, symbolizes the
rising sun of a new nation.

Night view of the United
Nations Headquarters
compound from
Roosevelt Island. Dubbed
the "workshop for peace"
by Director of Planning
Wallace K. Harrison, the
United Nations sends its
lights into the darkness.

The Capital Master Plan

**Secretary-General
of the United Nations**
Ban Ki-moon

Chef de Cabinet
Susana Malcorra

**Under-Secretary-General
for Management**
Yukio Takasu

**Assistant Secretary-General
for the Capital Master Plan**
Michael Adlerstein

Consultants
HLW International
Perkins+Will
Syska Hennessy Group

Di Domenico + Partners, LLP
Gardiner & Theobald
R. A. Heintges & Associates
Kroll Inc.
Weidlinger Associates, Inc.
Einhorn Yaffee Prescott Architecture
& Engineering, P.C.

Construction Manager
Skanska USA Building Inc.

United Nations Capital Master Plan Staff
Sarah Aguirre, Sevil Alirzayeva, April Almaria, Ozgur Altinoklar, Alvin Alunan, Rajan Ananthanarayanan, Princy Ariff, Helen Atuana, Mark Bandini, Gordon Bird, Patricia Burneo, Mark Camera, Ken Champion, Anjali Chhugani, Paul Choi, John Clarkson, Wally Clarkson, Simon Darnell, Sahra Diament, Renee Dua, Kathy Farbod, Kieran Fenichel, Maya Fridman, Susan Furmanski, Erin Gould, Katherine Grenier, Andrea Guzman, Noriyuki Hayashi, Charles Hill, Mark Hintzen, Jack Howard, Robert James Idea, Florin Ionescu, Nadira Kowlessar, Joanna Labos,

Karen Lee, Yaron Lubetzkey, Joseph Martella, James Massey, Joan McDonald, Marian Miszkiel, Colette Mninski, Sergio Moreno, Carlos Navarro, Toshiyuki Niwa, Daphnis Novoa, Mildred Ochoa, Assel Omarova-Reister, Simona Petrova-Vassileva, Charmaine Pieres, Louis Reuter IV, Jacqueline Rodin, Samantha Savarese, Corinna Schmidt, Werner Schmidt, Obin Silungwe, Peter Smith, Eugene Spiegle, Katya Tabourian, Om Taneja, Taline Tateossian, Vivian Van de Perre, Maria Vasquez, Lauraine Velez, Racquel Villanueva, Ana Villegas del Valle, Darren Walker, Keith Walton, Peter Wendeborn

The United Nations gratefully acknowledges the support of the United Nations Foundation for this book.

Under-Secretary-General Yukio Takasu, Secretary-General Ban Ki-moon, Chef de Cabinet Susana Malcorra, and Assistant Secretary-General Michael Adlerstein at the reopening of the renovated General Assembly Building, 15 September 2014.

Photography Credits

The United Nations is grateful to photographers Nancy Davenport, David Finn, William Rivelli, and Gary Rosenberg, who provided their images to the United Nations.

This book was created by the Office of the Capital Master Plan in cooperation with the Department of Public Information.